HOME and BACK

Grades 5 and 6

Bible Activities for Kids To Take and Return

Linda Washington

Rainbow Books

For my family and friends: Grace be unto you and peace through our Lord Jesus Christ.

HOME AND BACK FOR GRADES 5&6
©1999 by Rainbow Publishers
ISBN 1-885358-52-0
Rainbow reorder #RB36844

Rainbow Publishers
P.O. Box 261129
San Diego, CA 92196

Illustrator: Chuck Galey
Editor: Christy Allen

Printed in the United States of America

Contents

Introduction

Life after the lesson is a crucial part of every teacher's responsibility. You want to know that your children think about what you teach beyond the classroom. And you seek to encourage your students to return and to feel good about their experiences under your care and leadership. You also endeavor to instill a sense of belonging and self-worth in your kids.

Those ideals are exactly why *Home and Back* was created. With these 40 reproducible sheets, you can:
• extend the classroom lesson.
• promote attendance.
• celebrate holidays and events.
• share classroom news.

All with just one book! Not only are the sheets age-based and biblically sound, they present messages in exciting ways to capture your kids' attention. Rather than single-use postcards, *Home and Back* provides an activity for students to complete and return to class, encouraging children to maintain regular attendance. You only need to copy the sheet, fold it into thirds (use dashed guide lines on the back side), address and stamp. Staying in touch with your kids has never been easier!

Each book in this series includes sheets for a variety of Bible lessons that will complement your curriculum, as well as sheets for holidays, birthdays and other occasions. Blank invitations, suitable for class parties, are another convenient resource in the books. Answers to puzzles are on pages 93-96.

On the front of each self-mailing sheet is a full-page activity with a Bible verse. The back of the sheet has another activity or illustration, instructions to return the sheet for answers to puzzles and a section for the address and stamp. After you fill in the information, be sure to fold the sheet so the address faces outward, tape closed and add a stamp.

To get the most out of *Home and Back*, we recommend that you:

• Tell the students that you will be mailing a sheet to them so they can anticipate receiving it. Children love to get mail, especially from their teachers.
• Alternatively, consider distributing the sheets as the kids leave your classroom.
• Tear out the sheets at the perforations for easier copying.
• Write a personal note on each sheet.
• Encourage the children to memorize the Bible verse on the front of each sheet.
• Have small prizes on-hand to congratulate students who return their sheets.
• Use the sheets as a tool but not as your only communication with your students. Phone calls and personal visits are important.
• Keep a list of which sheets you send to students so you do not repeat them.

Whether you want to connect, care or communicate, you will soon find that *Home and Back* is the most effective way to reach your students. May God bless you as you seek to further His kingdom.

Old Testament

Lights, Camera, Creation!

Pretend you are a famous film director. It's your job to put together a video of what occurred on each day of Creation. Choose from the video stills below to fill in what happened on each day. Look up Genesis 1 if you need help. On the lines below, fill in the narration. What would you tell your audience about what happened?

Day 1:

_____

_____

Day 2:

_____

_____

Day 3:

_____

_____

Day 4:

_____

_____

Day 5:

_____

_____

Day 6:

_____

_____

God made the impossible possible by creating the world.

For nothing is impossible with God. Luke 1:37

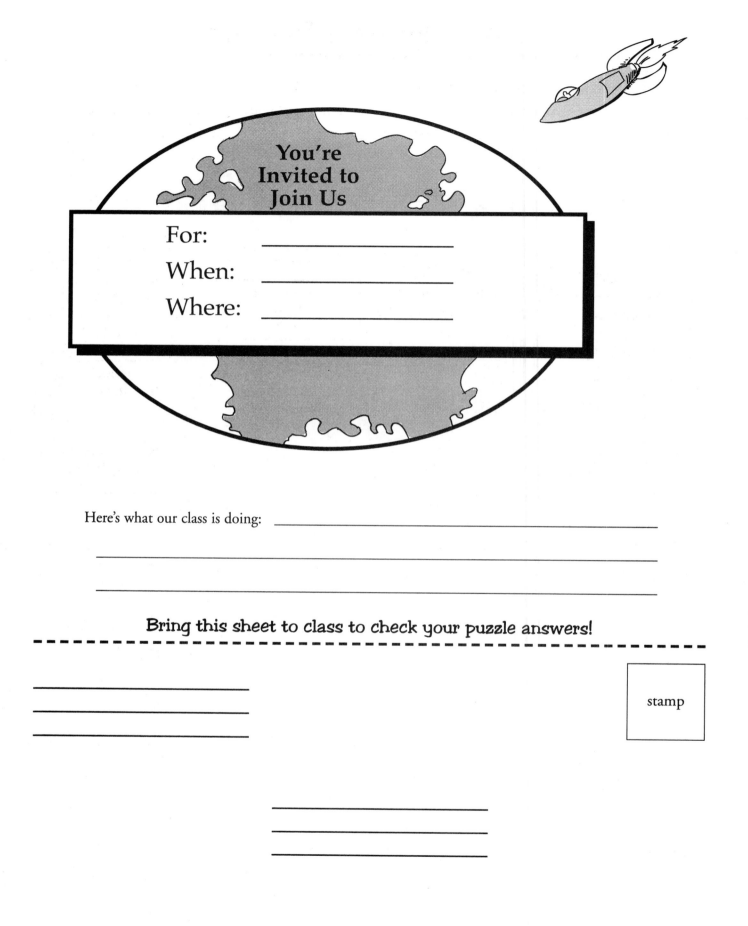

You're Invited to Join Us

For: _____

When: _____

Where: _____

Here's what our class is doing: _____

_____

_____

Bring this sheet to class to check your puzzle answers!

- -

_____

_____

_____

stamp

_____

_____

_____

Please Pass the Plagues!

In the scene below are the names of the ten plagues God placed on Egypt. Can you find all ten? If you're stumped, Exodus 7-12 will help. (Hint: One is not a plague!)

The plagues serve as a reminder that God is an awesome God.

How awesome is the Lord Most High, the great King over all the earth! Psalm 47:2

How Many?

There are a lot of numbers mentioned in the Bible. Each of the following questions can be answered with a number.

1 How many days did it rain while Noah and his family were in the ark? (Genesis 7:12)

2

2 How long did the Israelites wander in the desert? (Numbers 32:13)

How many men did Gideon take into battle against the Midianites? (Judges 7:8)

5

3 How many days of Creation were there? (Genesis 1:1-2:3) **6**

4

Here's what our class is doing: _____

_____

_____

Bring this sheet to class to check your puzzle answers!

- -

_____

_____

_____

stamp

_____

_____

_____

Old Testament Crossword

Many people had reason to praise God. Use the Scriptures to find each Old Testament person and fill in the crossword puzzle.

Across

1. He led the Israelites out of Egypt. (Exodus 14:1-11)
4. He wanted a son and he had one when he was 100. (Genesis 21:5)
5. This reluctant prophet ran to Tarshish instead of Nineveh. (Matthew 12:39-41)
6. He was anointed to become the king of Israel after Saul. (1 Samuel 16:1, 11-13)
8. He wouldn't go to battle without Deborah. (Judges 4:4-8)

Down

2. She was 90 when she had her first child. (Genesis 17:17)
3. He was jealous of David and tried to kill him. (1 Samuel 18:9)
4. He was Moses' brother and a high priest. (Exodus 4:14)
5. David's friend. (1 Samuel 19)
7. She was Moses' sister, a prophetess. (Exodus 15:20)

Come, let us sing for joy to the Lord; let us shout aloud to the Rock of our salvation.
Psalm 95:1

Bible Bowling

You get a pin for each person or thing you can name. If you name all ten in a category, you get a strike. If you have to look up the Scripture to find the answer, you get a spare. If you can remember part of the answer, give yourself a point for each correct answer.

Name ten of the twelve disciples. (Matthew 10:1-6)
_____
_____

Name the ten plagues God sent on Egypt during the time of Moses. (Exodus 7:17-11:7)
_____
_____

Name ten of the twelve tribes of Israel. (Numbers 1:20-44)
_____
_____

Name ten of the New Testament books.
_____
_____

Name ten Old Testament books. _____
_____

Name ten of Jesus' miracles. _____
_____

Here's what our class is doing: _____
_____
_____

Bring this sheet to class to check your puzzle answers!

- -

_____
_____
_____

stamp

_____
_____
_____

David: This Is Your Life!

Davidis one of the most interesting people in the Bible. His life was far from easy, however! Look at the items in this scrapbook of David's life. Each represents an event in his life. Identify what happened in each picture then write it below. The Scriptures in parentheses may help you.

Spear (1 Samuel 19:9-10) _____

My best friend and me (1 Samuel 20) _____

Saul's robe (1 Samuel 24:3-4) _____

My slingshot (1 Samuel 17) _____

Oil (1 Samuel 16) _____

Crown (2 Samuel 5:4) _____

I will sing praise to my God as long as I live. Psalm 104:33

Bible Bingo

Play Bible Bingo by yourself or with a friend. You can use coins for markers. Each of you should choose a symbol. Look up the Scriptures below. Each verse mentions something God either called Himself or provided for His people. If the verse or verses mentions the symbol you chose, place a coin over it. Whoever has three coins in a row has to call out BINGO to win. If you're playing alone, you still have to call out BINGO to win.

Shepherd   Water   Light   Bread

Bible Bingo

Psalm 23:1	Exodus 16:4	John 8:12
John 10:11	John 6:35	John 4:14
Exodus 17:6	2 Corinthians 11:23-24	Exodus 13:21

Here's what our class is doing: _____

_____

_____

Bring this sheet to class to check your puzzle answers!

- -

_____

_____

_____

stamp

_____

_____

_____

Past Playback

Did you ever rewind a tape or video to replay a scene or piece of music? Sometimes it is necessary to make sure you've heard everything correctly. Check out each panel below. The scenes show how God called Moses to go to Pharaoh. Is each scene correct? You'll need to hit the rewind button to make sure you have the story straight. If it is, write yes below the picture. If not, write why it is wrong.

A lake is on fire! I think I'll get closer to find out why.

PLAYBACK!

Is this what happened? See Exodus 3:1-3. _____

_____

My cloak has turned into a snake!

PLAYBACK!

Is this what happened? See Exodus 4:1-5. _____

_____

Bible Words

See if you can unscramble these words connected to Moses and the Israelites. If you're too stumped, you can look up the Scriptures for help.

 HIDIMREP   This is the place where the Israelites camped and quarreled over water. God gave them water from a rock. (Exodus 17:1-7)

 NANAM   This is the bread God gave the Israelites to eat. The word means "What is it?" (Exodus 16:31-36)

 TEHORJ   This man was Moses' father-in-law, who came for a visit. (Exodus 18:1-5)

 **NAISI**   The mountain where the Israelites journeyed after leaving Egypt. (Exodus 19:17-23)

 **BATERNALCE**   This is the tent where the Israelites worshiped God. (Exodus 25:9–26:1; 40:1, 2)

Here's what our class is doing: _____

_____

_____

Bring this sheet to class to check your puzzle answers!

- -

_____

_____

_____

stamp

_____

_____

_____

Words to Remember

Use the code to find good advice from Proverbs 3:5. Each symbol represents a letter of the alphabet. Pay attention to the way each letter looks in the code box. Fill in the blanks with each correct letter. Memorize it!

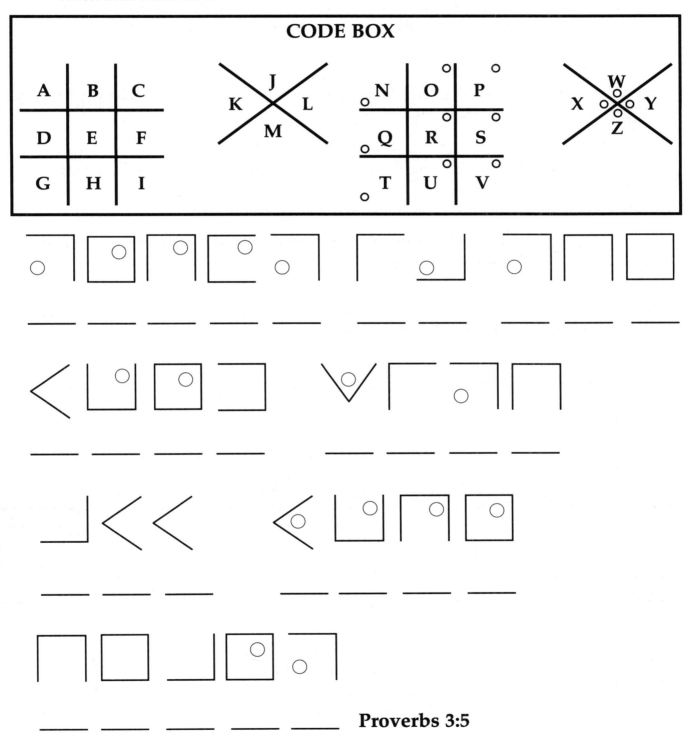

Proverbs 3:5

A Message for You

Hold the sheet so that the bottom of the paper is close to your eyes to read the first part of the message. Turn the sheet horizontally to read the second part.

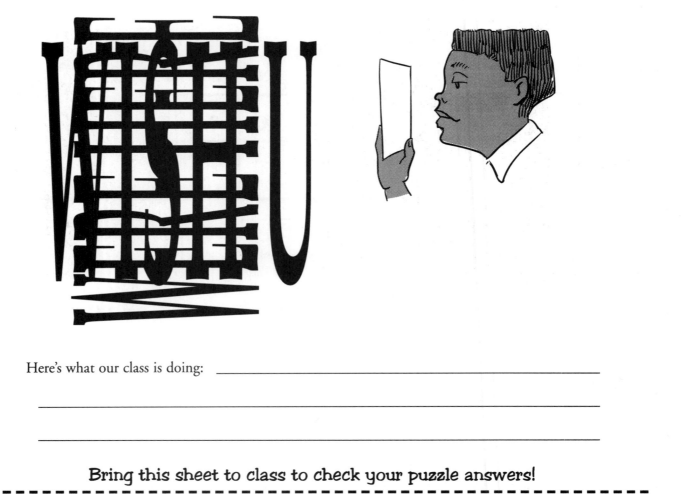

Here's what our class is doing: _____

_____

_____

Bring this sheet to class to check your puzzle answers!

- -

_____

_____

_____

stamp

_____

_____

_____

Attention Grabber

King Belshazzar robbed the temple of Jerusalem. So God did something unusual to get Belshazzar's attention. To find out what God did, hold the message below up to a mirror. For the whole story, read Daniel 5.

Connect a Word

Try to form words of three or more letters out of the grid below. Words can be formed diagonally, across, up or down. For example: RAY (see below). Proper names don't count! The letters you use must be connected somehow. You cannot skip over letters to form words.

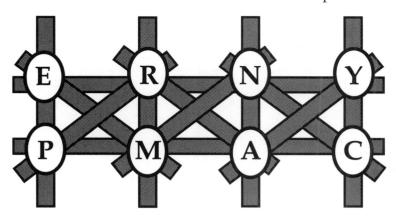

_____

_____

A gentle answer turns away wrath, but a harsh word stirs up anger. Proverbs 15:1

Choose Wise Words

A word can make or break someone's day. You can choose to be gentle as the memory verse explains. Choose some of the words you formed in the puzzle on the front. Write a message on the T-shirt to help someone who is having a bad day.

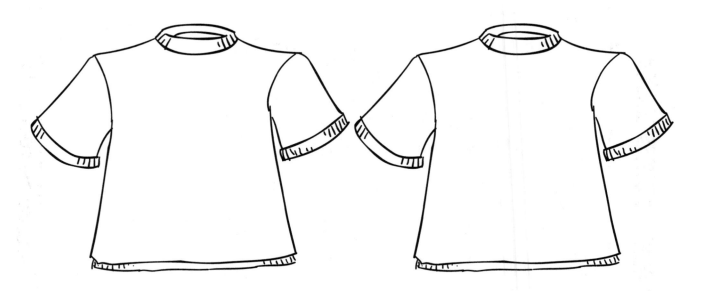

Here's what our class is doing: _____

_____

_____

Bring this sheet to class to check your puzzle answers!

- -

_____

_____

_____

stamp

_____

_____

_____

Prophets of God

God called many men and women to speak His Word. See if you can find the prophets of God listed below in this word search.

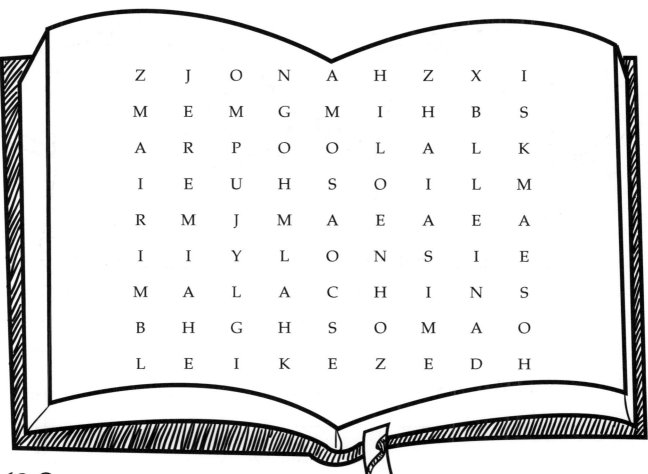

Z	J	O	N	A	H	Z	X	I
M	E	M	G	M	I	H	B	S
A	R	P	O	O	L	A	L	K
I	E	U	H	S	O	I	L	M
R	M	J	M	A	E	A	E	A
I	I	Y	L	O	N	S	I	E
M	A	L	A	C	H	I	N	S
B	H	G	H	S	O	M	A	O
L	E	I	K	E	Z	E	D	H

Amos	Hosea	Jeremiah	Malachi	Moses
Daniel	Isaiah	Jonah	Miriam	Zephaniah
Ezekiel				

What other names of Bible prophets do you know? _____

_____

_____

Do not touch my anointed ones; do my prophets no harm. 1 Chronicles 16:22

Word Break

Take a word break with this puzzle.

How many words of three or more letters can you make out of the word

Christianity?

Names like "Christ" and "Chris" do not count. _____

_____

_____

_____

_____

_____

_____

Here's what our class is doing: _____

_____

_____

Bring this sheet to class to check your puzzle answers!

- -

_____

_____

_____

stamp

_____

_____

_____

New Testament

Bible Baseball: Miracles of Jesus

Baseball season is here! Wait, put down that bat! Your knowledge of Jesus' miracles can help you score points. Look at the scorecard below. Each question you answer correctly will put you on first, second or third base. If you answer four questions correctly, you score a home run. How many home runs can you score? Look up the Scripture after each question if you need help.

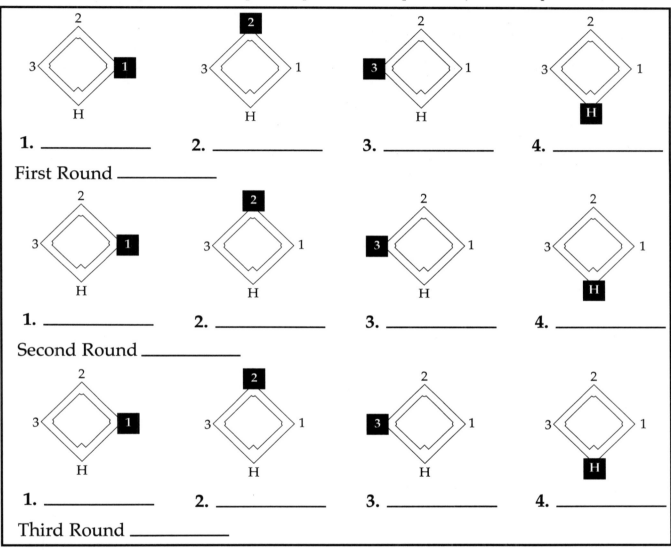

1. _____ 2. _____ 3. _____ 4. _____

First Round _____

1. _____ 2. _____ 3. _____ 4. _____

Second Round _____

1. _____ 2. _____ 3. _____ 4. _____

Third Round _____

Questions

1. What did Jesus use to turn into wine? (John 2:1-11)
2. What did the centurion ask Jesus to do? (Matthew 8:5-13; Luke 7:1-10)
3. Why did the Pharisees get mad at Jesus for healing a man with a withered hand? (Matthew 12:9-13)
4. What did the Canaanite woman want Jesus to do? (Mark 7:24-30)
5. Jesus healed a man at Bethsaida. What was the man's problem? (Mark 8:22-26)
6. What did Jesus do with five loaves and two fish? (Luke 9:12-17)
7. How did the friends of a paralyzed man get him to Jesus? (Mark 2:1-12)
8. Jesus met a sad widow at Nain. What did he do for her? (Luke 7:11-15)
9. Jesus surprised His disciples one night when he did this miraculous thing on water. (Mark 6:48-51)
10. The disciples were terrified one night while in a boat. Jesus did this to help them feel better. (Mark 4:37-41)
11. Ten men with leprosy went to Jesus for help. How many thanked Him for the healing they received? (Luke 17:11-19)
12. Where did Jesus heal a man who had been sick for 38 years? (John 5:1-9)

Mystery Code

Use the code to figure out the memory verse Hebrews 13:8. Some of the letters in the code grid are not used.

☞	✓	⊹	♣	♠	◆	◇	★	✚	✪	✩	★	✐
A	B	C	D	E	F	G	H	I	J	K	L	M

✍	➡	☆	✳	✖	✳	❋	✶	❀	⊛			
N	O	P	R	S	T	U	V	Y	Z			

✪ ♠ ✖ ❋ ✖   ⊹ ★ ✳ ✚ ✖ ❋
___ ___ ___ ___ ___   ___ ___ ___ ___ ___ ___

✚ ✖   ✳ ★ ♠   ✖ ☞ ✐ ♠
___ ___   ___ ___ ___   ___ ___ ___ ___

❀ ♠ ✖ ✳ ♠ ✳ ♣ ☞ ❀   ☞ ✍ ♣
___ ___ ___ ___ ___ ___ ___ ___ ___   ___ ___ ___

✳ ➡ ♣ ☞ ❀   ☞ ✍ ♣
___ ___ ___ ___ ___   ___ ___ ___

◆ ➡ ✳ ♠ ✶ ♠ ✳
___ ___ ___ ___ ___ ___ ___   Hebrews 13:8

Here's what our class is doing: _____

_____

Bring this sheet to class to check your puzzle answers!

- -

_____
_____
_____

stamp

_____
_____
_____

28

Look Closely

Look at the picture below for one minute. Then turn this sheet over. See how many details you can remember.

Pay Attention!

Jesus talked a lot about the importance of paying attention. One thing He said over and over was "He who has ears to hear, let him hear." In Matthew 6:19-34, He gives us a list of Do's and Don'ts to follow. To see if you're paying attention to what He says, fill in the chart below. What should we do? What shouldn't we do?

Do

_____

_____

_____

Don't

_____

_____

_____

Be alert and always keep on praying for all the saints. Ephesians 6:18

What Do You Remember?

Answer the questions to see how much you remember about the scene on the front. (No peeking!)

1. What was on the bed? _____

   _____

2. What was on the floor behind the cat?

   a. train track   b. racing car set _____

3. What pattern was on the rug: a diamond or a square? _____

4. Where were the skates? _____

   Here's what our class is doing: _____

   _____

   _____

- -

_____

_____

_____

stamp

_____

_____

_____

The Perils of Paul

The apostle Paul got into a number of sticky situations on his missionary journeys. See if you can lend him a hand by solving each puzzle.

1. One night, Paul had a vision. Where did he go? Macedonia or Antioch? (Acts 16:9)

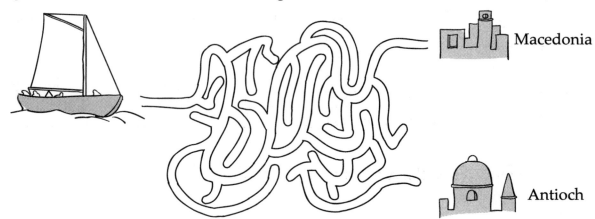

Macedonia

Antioch

2. Paul and other missionaries traveled to many places to preach the Gospel. Look up the scriptures below to find each place where Paul traveled. After you fill in each word, put each numbered letter in the proper box below to complete some advice for anyone facing a sticky situation.

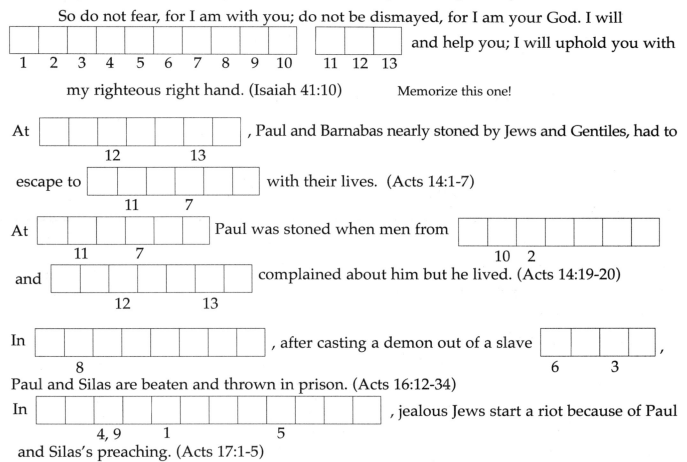

So do not fear, for I am with you; do not be dismayed, for I am your God. I will

| | | | | | | | | | | | | | | | | | | |

1 2 3 4 5 6 7 8 9 10   11 12 13

and help you; I will uphold you with

my righteous right hand. (Isaiah 41:10)   Memorize this one!

At [   ] , Paul and Barnabas nearly stoned by Jews and Gentiles, had to

12   13

escape to [   ] with their lives. (Acts 14:1-7)

11   7

At [   ] Paul was stoned when men from [   ]

11   7   10 2

and [   ] complained about him but he lived. (Acts 14:19-20)

12   13

In [   ] , after casting a demon out of a slave [   ] ,

8   6   3

Paul and Silas are beaten and thrown in prison. (Acts 16:12-34)

In [   ] , jealous Jews start a riot because of Paul

4,9   1   5

and Silas's preaching. (Acts 17:1-5)

Concentration

Play a version of the game Concentration. Read the list below. Find the two items or people that go together.

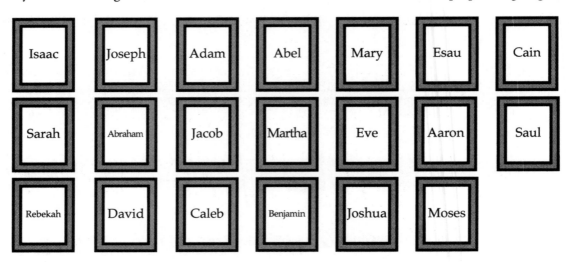

- The first man and woman (Genesis 3:20)
- This son of Abraham married this sister of Laban (Genesis 24:66-67)
- This brother killed the other (Genesis 4:8)
- This elderly couple had a baby (Genesis 21:1-2)
- These two were Rachel's sons (Genesis 30:22-24; 35:16-18)
- These two spies were the only ones who were excited about the promised land (Numbers 14:6-7)
- These men were Miriam's two brothers (Numbers 26:59)
- These sisters of Lazarus went to Jesus when their brother was sick (John 11:1-2)
- The first two kings of Israel (1 Samuel 10:1, 18-21; 2 Samuel 16:1, 12-13)

Here's what our class is doing: _____

_____

Bring this sheet to class to check your puzzle answers!

_____

_____

_____

stamp

_____

_____

_____

Extra! Extra!

What has God done for you that you'd like to tell someone else about? Fill in the newspaper story with the facts.

Daily Blabber

_____

_____

_____

_____

_____

_____

_____

_____

I am not ashamed of the gospel, because it is the power of God for the salvation of everyone who believes: first for the Jew, then for the Gentile. Romans 1:16

Cool Acrostic

Whats cool about being part of God's family? You decide! Fill in the acrostic with words that describe how you feel about being a Christian.

C _____

O _____

O _____

L _____

Here's what our class is doing: _____

_____

_____

Bring this sheet to class to check your puzzle answers!

_____

_____

_____

stamp

_____

_____

_____

The Resurrection

A lot of events happened after the Resurrection. See if you can find the people or items involved just by reading the clues. Names can be found across, down, diagonally or backward.

1. This land hazard happened at Jesus' death and resurrection (Matthew 28:2).
2. She saw the risen Savior at the tomb (John 20:10-18).
3. This disciple was asked the same question three times by the risen Lord (John 21:15-17).
4. This disciple was the first one to enter the tomb (John 20:4).
5. The two disciples found this in the tomb (John 20:6-7).
6. This disciple doubted that Jesus was alive (John 20:24-28).
7. Women saw this at the tomb (Matthew 28:5).
8. The women at the tomb wondered who rolled away this item (Mark 16:1-3).
9. These people were terrified when they saw a strange being appear at the tomb (Matthew 28:4).
10. On the road to this village, two disciples saw the risen Lord (Luke 24:13).

T	O	G	O	D	P	E	T	E	R	W
H	T	O	L	C	L	A	I	R	U	B
O	H	O	L	Y	M	R	A	J	A	M
G	O	D	Z	M	S	T	O	N	E	K
T	M	G	A	S	M	H	O	L	Y	N
M	A	U	N	U	N	Q	N	Y	V	X
B	S	A	W	A	E	U	R	Z	O	O
J	A	R	R	M	W	A	N	G	E	L
L	A	D	E	M	M	K	N	O	W	S
I	S	S	U	E	D	E	F	O	R	E

I am the resurrection and the life. He who believes in me will live, even though he dies; and whoever lives and believes in me will never die. John 11:25-26

From Death to Life

Easter is a time for transformation. Because of Jesus' death, we can have eternal life. See if you can transform the word DEATH into LIFE just by changing, adding or dropping one letter each time you form a new word. The first word has been done for you. Then try your hand at changing each of the top words into their opposites. (Hints: The number of blanks gives you the number of letters in each word. You may have to shuffle a few letters around to form words.)

DEATH
HEATH
_ _ _ _ _
_ _ _ _ _
_ _ _ _ _
_ _ _ _ _
_ _ _ _ _
_ _ _ _ _
_ _ _ _ _
LIFE

SOUR
_ _ _ _
_ _ _ _
_ _ _ _
_ _ _ _
_ _ _ _
_ _ _ _ _
SWEET

EARLY
_ _ _ _
_ _ _ _ _ _
_ _ _ _
_ _ _ _
LATE

Here's what our class is doing: _____

_____

_____

Bring this sheet to class to check your puzzle answers!

_____

_____

_____

stamp

_____

_____

_____

They Played a Part

There were many people connected with Jesus' arrest, betrayal and crucifixion. Use the Scripture to fill in each person's name in the puzzle below.

ACROSS

1. I denied Him three times.
   (Matthew 26:69-70)
2. I was released from prison, while He was led to His death.
   (Matthew 27:21)
5. I betrayed Him for thirty pieces of silver. (Matthew 27:3)

DOWN

1. I found nothing wrong with Him, but still allowed Him to be crucified. (John 18:38)
3. I washed His feet before He died.
   (John 12:3-7)
4. I tried Jesus before sending Him to the Roman governor.
   (Matthew 26:57)

And they crucified him. Mark 15:24

The Reason for the Season

For whom did Jesus die? Color the spaces that have sums that add up to 4.

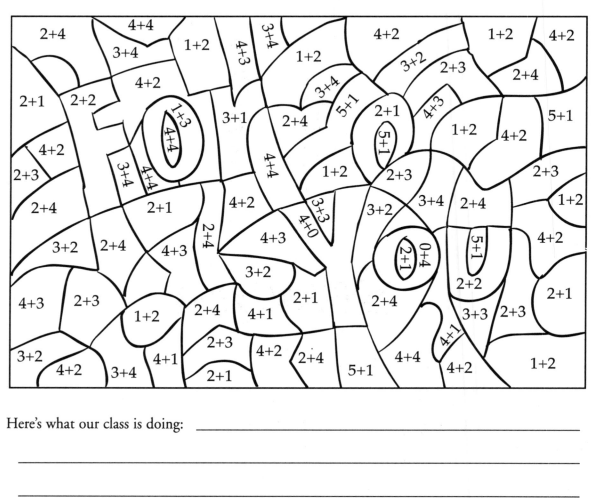

Here's what our class is doing: _____

_____

_____

Bring this sheet to class to check your puzzle answers!

- -

_____

_____

_____

stamp

_____

_____

_____

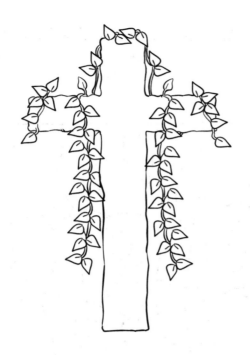

Seasonal

Winter Wonderland

Isn't winter wonderful? Some winter scenes, like the one below, show the wonder of winter. But wait! The same scene is shown twice. But there are some changes between Scene 1 and Scene 2. How many can you spot?

Scene 1

Scene 2

If anyone serves, he should do it with the strength God provides. 1 Peter 4:11

Whiling Away Winter

Are you worried as you wonder what ways you can while away winter? (Try saying that ten times fast!) Wonder no more! Use the acrostic below to make your plans. Using each letter of the word WINTER, write some ways you can spend your time serving God this winter. For example: "W—Write a note to my pastor to tell him he's doing a great job."

W _____

I _____

N _____

T _____

E _____

R _____

Here's what our class is doing: _____

_____

_____

Bring this sheet to class to check your puzzle answers!

- -

_____

_____

_____

stamp

_____

_____

_____

Plenty of Love

In honor of Valentine's Day, here is a Bible verse that has plenty of love. Find each letter by adding the numbers underneath each heart. Match the sum you get with the sum underneath each letter. The first one has been done for you. Memorize it!

A	B	C	D	E	F	G	H	I	J	K	L	M
2	3	4	6	11	15	7	9	12	5	8	1	17

N	O	P	Q	R	S	T	U	V	W	X	Y	Z
14	16	24	19	21	18	20	23	22	10	30	13	25

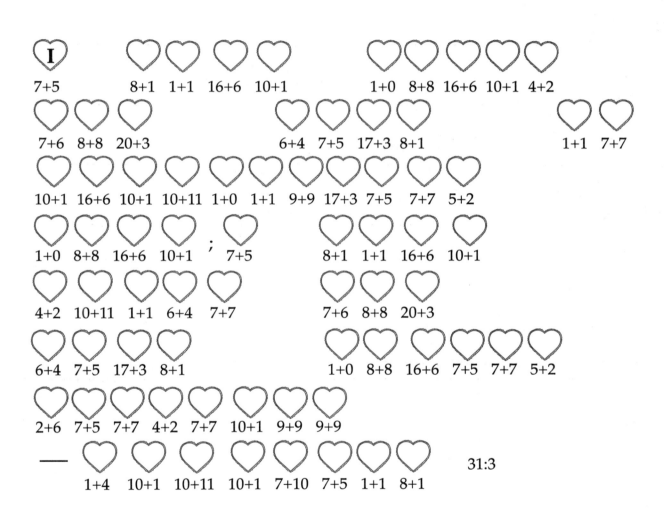

But the greatest of these is love. 1 Corinthians 13:13

The Ultimate Love

First Corinthians 13 is called "the love chapter." How can you use the advice from this chapter to show love to others?

Love is patient, love is kind. It does not envy, it does not boast, it is not proud.

It is not rude, it is not self-seeking, it is not easily angered, it keeps no record of wrongs.

Love does not delight in evil but rejoices with the truth.

It always protects, always trusts, always hopes, always perseveres.

Love never fails. But where there are prophecies, they will cease; where there are tongues, they will be stilled; where there is knowledge, it will pass away. And now these three remain: faith, hope and love.

Here's what our class is doing: _____

_____

_____

Bring this sheet to class to check your puzzle answers!

- -

_____

_____

_____

stamp

_____

_____

_____

Bible "Jeopardy"

It's time to play a form of the popular game Jeopardy. The category is Jesus and the Samaritan Woman at the Well. Think you know the story pretty well? We'll see! The answers are given below. All you have to do is supply the questions or the comment that caused the remark to be made. Easy, huh? If you're unsure, check the Scriptures. Here's an example to get you started:

Answer: "You're a Samaritan. I'm a Jew." (John 4:7-8)
Question/Comment: "Will you give me a drink?"

Answer: "If you knew who asks you for a drink, you'd ask me for living water." (John 4:9-10)
Question/Comment: _____

Answer: "The water I will give will become a spring of water." (John 4:11-12)
Question/Comment: _____

Answer: "I have no husband." (John 4:16-17)
Question/Comment: _____

Answer: "I who speak to you am he." (John 4:25-26)
Question/Comment: _____

What did the woman decide to do? _____

Bonus Round: The answer is given in the Bible verse below. Can you think of a question that goes with it? _____

If anyone is in Christ, he is a new creation;
the old has gone, the new has come! 2 Corinthians 5:17

45

Spring Changes

Now that the season has changed to spring, a few other changes are necessary. See if you can change WINTER to SPRING, and SEED to PLANT just by changing a letter at a time. (For WINTER, you'll have to change two letters in two instances.) The clues will help.

WINTER

_ _ _ _ _ _   Someone who comes in first place.
_ _ _ _ _ _   Someone who breaks God's law.
_ _ _ _ _ _ _   Something you twirl when playing a board game.
_ _ _ _ _ _ _ _   A small piece of wood under your skin.
_ _ _ _ _ _   What is placed over a broken bone.
_ _ _ _ _ _   A quick run.

SPRING

SEED

_ _ _ _   A plant along the riverbank.
_ _ _ _   What you do with a book.
_ _ _ _   The tip of a pencil.
_ _ _ _ _   Another word for beg.
_ _ _ _ _   Kilts have this pattern.
_ _ _ _ _   The opposite of fancy.

PLANT

Here's what our class is doing: _____

_____

_____

Bring this sheet to class to check your puzzle answers!

- -

_____

_____

_____

stamp

_____

_____

_____

Independence Day

This news station has a major story straight out of Daniel 3. In that chapter, Shadrach, Meshach and Abednego declared their independence from the king's law. But are the facts correct? You can decide whether they need to be edited. If they are accurate, circle the green light button. If not, check the edit button, then rewrite the fact.

How did the story end? Write about it or draw pictures of it in the blank video screens on the back of this sheet.

Jesus said, "For it is written: 'Worship the Lord your God, and serve him only.'" Matthew 4:10

Summer Fun

What are your plans for the summer? _____

_____

_____

Here's what our class is doing: _____

_____

_____

Bring this sheet to class to check your puzzle answers!

- -

_____

_____

_____

stamp

_____

_____

_____

Back to the Book

The Israelites had returned from Babylon, the land of their captivity. Nehemiah had helped them rebuild the walls of Jerusalem. Now they had more they needed to learn. Fill in the crossword puzzle to learn the details of Nehemiah 8.

Across

1. _____, the governor of the land, asked the man of number 2 down to read to the people (8:9).

6. The man of number 2 down made what he read seem very _____— easy to understand (8:8).

7. The man of 2 down worked as a _____. That meant he could offer sacrifices (8:2).

9. The man of 2 down read the _____ of Moses to the people (8:3).

10. God's Word was known as the _____ of the (9 across) (8:3).

Down

2. This man was asked to read God's Word to the people of 3 down (8:1).

3. These people were the twelve tribes of _____ (8:1).

4. The people met at this place to hear God's Word (8:3).

5. The man of 2 down also had this job (8:1).

8. The people didn't sit, they _____ all morning listening to the Word (8:5).

11. The people were on their feet from morning till _____ (8:3).

Do your best to present yourself to God as one approved, a workman who does not need to be ashamed and who correctly handles the word of truth. 2 Timothy 2:15

Heads Up!

All of the word groups and pictures below represent common phrases that contain the word "head." Look at each picture carefully. Can you figure out each phrase? If so, you're a "HEAD" of the game!

HEAD (in clouds)

1.

HEAD
HEELS **IN LOVE**

2.

A GOOD HEAD
YOUR SHOULDERS

3.

Keep your head

4.

Over I your N head

5.

4 the

6.

Aa Bb Cc

yoIt'sur heallad

7.

8. **AT THE**

Here's what our class is doing: _____

_____

Bring this sheet to class to check your puzzle answers!

- -

_____
_____
_____

stamp

_____
_____
_____

Man Overboard!

The people below on the left side have found themselves in some very uncomfortable places. Match the person to a common phrase on the right that you think fits what happened to the person. If you need help, look up the Scriptures next to their names. Warning: Some of the phrases don't match the people! For each correct answer, give yourself the points listed by each phrase. (If you look up the passage to find the answer, you only get 1 point per answer.)

1. Eutychus (Acts 20:7-12)

2. Jonah (Jonah 1:3-17)

3. Jeremiah (Jeremiah 38:6)

4. Daniel (Daniel 6:16-17)

5. Paul (Acts 27:36-44)

A. Well, well, well   10 points

B. Kitty corner   5 points

C. Into the wild blue yonder
   10 points

D. He fell for it   25 points

E. Into the deep blue sea
   10 points

F. If I were stranded on a
   desert island…   10 points

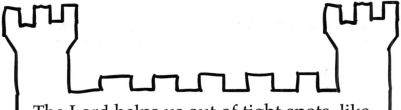

The Lord helps us out of tight spots, like He helped the men above. When we're afraid because of rough circumstances, here's something we can remember.

The Lord is my light and my salvation — whom shall I fear? The Lord is the stronghold of my life — of whom shall I be afraid? Psalm 27:1

Fall

Fall has arrived! In honor of the season, here's a little activity. How many times does the word fall appear below?

FALLFALLFAILFALLFALLFALFOLLFALLFALLFILLFALL
FALLFALLFALALFYLLFULLFALLFALLFALLFALLFALA
FALLFAILFALLFALLFALLFALLFALLFALLFALLFALALFOIL

Here's what our class is doing: _____

_____

_____

Bring this sheet to class to check your puzzle answers!

_____

_____

_____

stamp

_____

_____

_____

A Thankful Heart

Thanksgiving is a special time for giving thanks to God. The people below had a lot for which to be thankful. Use the code to figure out for what each person was thankful. Then read the stories in your Bible.

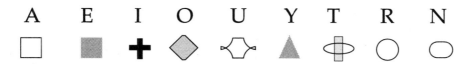

A   E   I   O   U   Y   T   R   N

one leper (Luke 17:11-19)

H ▣ ☐ L ✚ ◯ G   (HEALING)

Solomon (1 Kings 8:54-64)

⊕ ▣ M P L ▣   (TEMPLE)

Jacob (Genesis 28:10-17)

G ◈ D'S   P ◯ ▣ S ◯ C ▣   (GOD'S PRESENCE)

Anna & Simeon (Luke 2:25-38)

M ▣ S S ✚ ☐ H   (MESSIAH)

David (2 Samuel 6:1-15)

◯ ▣ ⊕ ⬙ ◯ ◯   ◈ F   ⊕ H ▣   ☐ ◯ K   (RETURN OF THE ARK)

Let everything that has breath praise the Lord. Praise the Lord. Psalm 150:6

Psalms of Thanks

Psalm 150

1. Praise the Lord. Praise God in his sanctuary; praise him in his mighty heavens.

2. Praise him for his acts of power; praise him for his surpassing greatness.

3. Praise him with the sounding of the trumpet, praise him with the harp and lyre,

4. Praise him with tambourine and dancing, praise him with the strings and flute,

5. Praise him with the clash of cymbals, praise him with resounding cymbals.

6. Let everything that has breath praise the Lord. Praise the Lord.

Your Psalm of Praise
What are you thankful for? Fill in a word or phrase that begins with each letter.

T _____

H _____

A _____

N _____

K _____

S _____

Here's what our class is doing: _____

_____

_____

Bring this sheet to class to check your puzzle answers!

_____
_____
_____

stamp

_____
_____
_____

A Christmas Gift

God has a gift for you, just waiting to be opened. The gift is disguised as the message on this box. To find the message, copy every other letter, starting at the T. Go around the box twice, then follow the arrow to the second row. Beginning at the B, copy every other letter. You'll find a message from Luke 2:11.

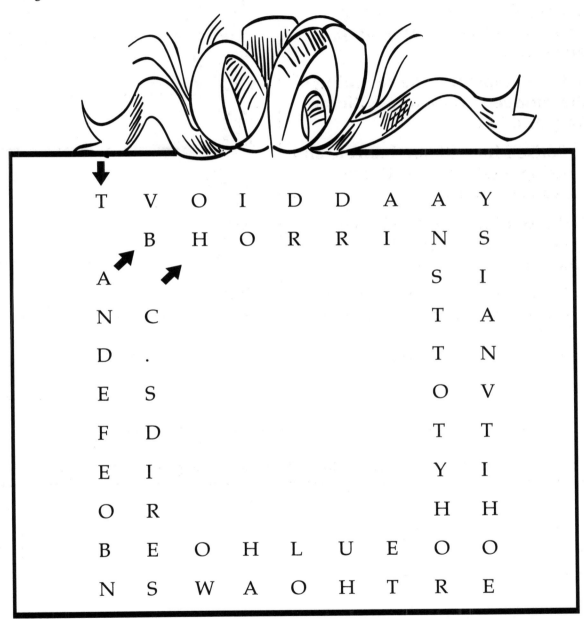

_____

_____. Luke 2:11

The Gift Exchange

The kids in this Sunday school class exchanged names to give each other gifts. Use the clue in each picture to figure out which kid gave which gift below. Can you figure out who gave what? Draw a line between the correct pairs.

Here's what our class is doing: _____

_____

_____

Bring this sheet to class to check your puzzle answers!

stamp

Searching for the Savior

Can you help the wise men get to Herod in Jerusalem, visit the child Jesus in Bethlehem and out again?

OUT

Glory to God in the highest, and on earth peace to men on whom his favor rests. Luke 2:14

Planning for Peace

What would you like to do to bring glory to God in the new year? Fill in the ornaments with your plans for carrying out the Bible verse on front.

Here's what our class is doing: _____

_____

_____

Bring this sheet to class to check your puzzle answers!

stamp

Year-Round

Who's Hospitable?

Think of someone who made you feel especially welcome when you entered his or her home. What did that person do to make you feel welcome? Look at the names below. Some of these Old Testament people helped others to feel welcome, or were helpful in some way. Others weren't. Who deserves a good housekeeping award? Cast your vote for "the host with the most" by putting a check mark in the hospitable column.

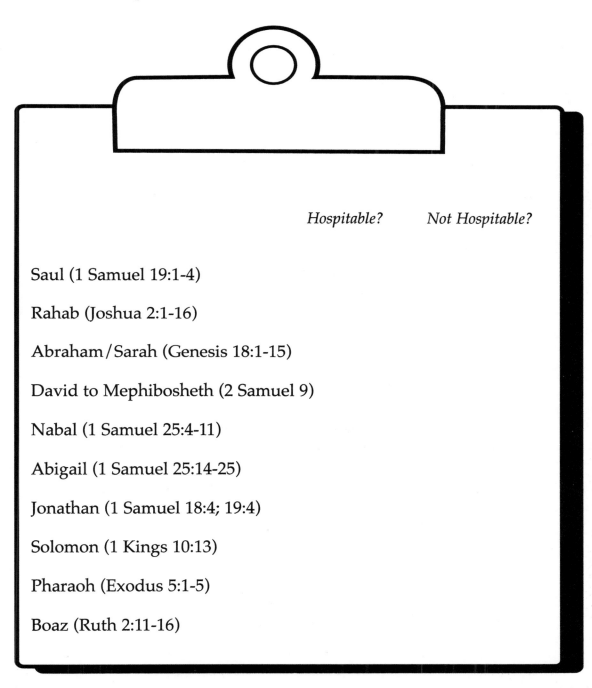

	Hospitable?	Not Hospitable?
Saul (1 Samuel 19:1-4)		
Rahab (Joshua 2:1-16)		
Abraham/Sarah (Genesis 18:1-15)		
David to Mephibosheth (2 Samuel 9)		
Nabal (1 Samuel 25:4-11)		
Abigail (1 Samuel 25:14-25)		
Jonathan (1 Samuel 18:4; 19:4)		
Solomon (1 Kings 10:13)		
Pharaoh (Exodus 5:1-5)		
Boaz (Ruth 2:11-16)		

Above all, love each other deeply, because love covers over a multitude of sins. Offer hospitality to one another without grumbling. 1 Peter 4:8-9

You're Welcome

WE WANT YOU

To come to:
❑ **a worship service**
❑ **Sunday school**
❑ **other**
Where: _____
When: _____

We want you to feel welcome whenever you come. Please come again.

Here's what our class is doing: _____

_____

_____

Bring this sheet to class to check your puzzle answers!

- -

_____

_____

_____

| stamp |

_____

_____

_____

Special Delivery

These people had special babies born to them. Match the parents to the offspring and write the number of the couple after the answer. Be warned! One statement is true for two sets of parents!

1. Abraham and Sarah

2. Adam and Eve

3. Isaac and Rebekah

4. Jacob and Rachel

5. Mary and Joseph

A. Our son grew up to be the Savior of the world. _____

B. We had two boys! We just wish they wouldn't fight so much! _____

C. Our son was sold as a slave in Egypt. Later he became an important man there. _____

D. Finally we had a boy! It took forever, though! We were old when we had him. _____

O Lord, you have searched me and you know me. You know when I sit and when I rise; you perceive my thoughts from afar. You discern my going out and my lying down; you are familiar with all my ways. Psalm 139:1-3

You Are Special

Today is your special day! That's why we're sending you these birthday greetings.

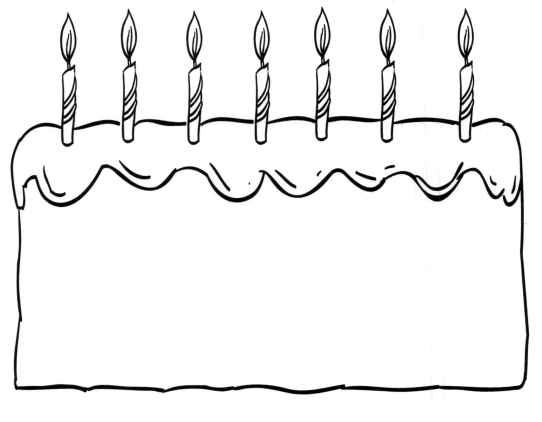

Here's what our class is doing: _____

_____

_____

Bring this sheet to class to check your puzzle answers!

- -

_____

_____

_____

stamp

_____

_____

_____

Rx for What Ails You

A sickness requires a certain medication — one made especially to cure that illness. The pain and hurt we feel or cause others need to be cured, too. See if you can match the cure with the sickness. Draw a line between them.

Let him who boasts boast in the Lord.
1 Corinthians 1:31

I will never leave you nor forsake you.
Joshua 1:5

A gentle answer turns away wrath, but a harsh word stirs up anger.
Proverbs 15:1

Nobody cares about me.

Why are you always using my stuff? Get out!

I have the best grade in the whole class.

God is our refuge and strength, an ever-present help in trouble. Psalm 46:1

Bull's-Eye!

Here's a game you can play while you wait to get well. With this game you decide which questions you'll answer. Each category of question is worth a certain amount of points. Easy:25, Medium Hard:50, Super Hard:75 or Impossible:150. Ask a friend to play. You choose the type of question your opponent will answer and vice versa.

Questions

Easy
Who betrayed Jesus?
Who were the first man and woman?
From which tree in the Garden of Eden were the first people told not to eat?

Medium Hard
Who cut off the high priest's servant's ear?
What was Cain's occupation before he killed Abel?
Against what nation did God send Gideon?

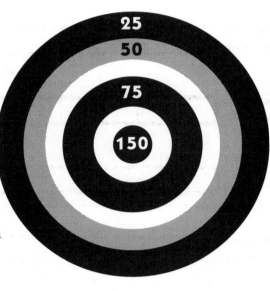

Super Hard
What is the name of the high priest's servant who lost an ear?
What two things did Gideon and his 300 men take into battle?

Impossible (check your Bible!)
Who were the two men who didn't die but were just taken away?

Here's what our class is doing: _____

_____

_____

Bring this sheet to class to check your puzzle answers!

_____

_____

_____

stamp

_____

_____

_____

Hospitality, New Testament Style

Some people know how to roll out the red carpet when it comes to making people feel welcome. Their attitudes seem to say: "Come on in. Make yourself at home." In each of the stories below, who is giving service with a smile? Who isn't? Mark the "Attitude-ometer" by shading it in for each attitude: cold, warmer or warm. A "warm host" would be shaded in completely.

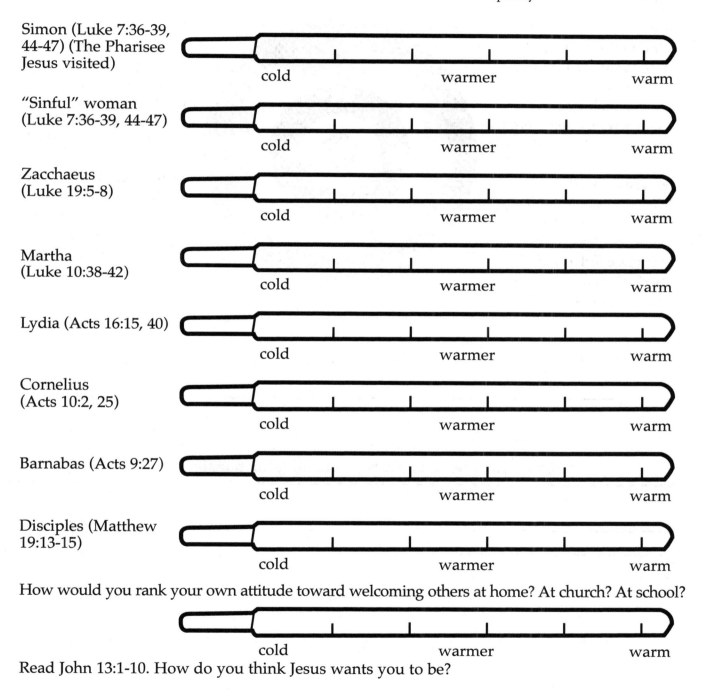

Simon (Luke 7:36-39, 44-47) (The Pharisee Jesus visited)

"Sinful" woman (Luke 7:36-39, 44-47)

Zacchaeus (Luke 19:5-8)

Martha (Luke 10:38-42)

Lydia (Acts 16:15, 40)

Cornelius (Acts 10:2, 25)

Barnabas (Acts 9:27)

Disciples (Matthew 19:13-15)

How would you rank your own attitude toward welcoming others at home? At church? At school?

Read John 13:1-10. How do you think Jesus wants you to be?

Here's a welcome from Jesus, the ultimate "host with the most":

Come to me, all you who are weary and burdened, and I will give you rest. Matthew 11:28

An Important Message

Here is a message for you, but each word has a wrong letter. It's up to you to find out what's what.

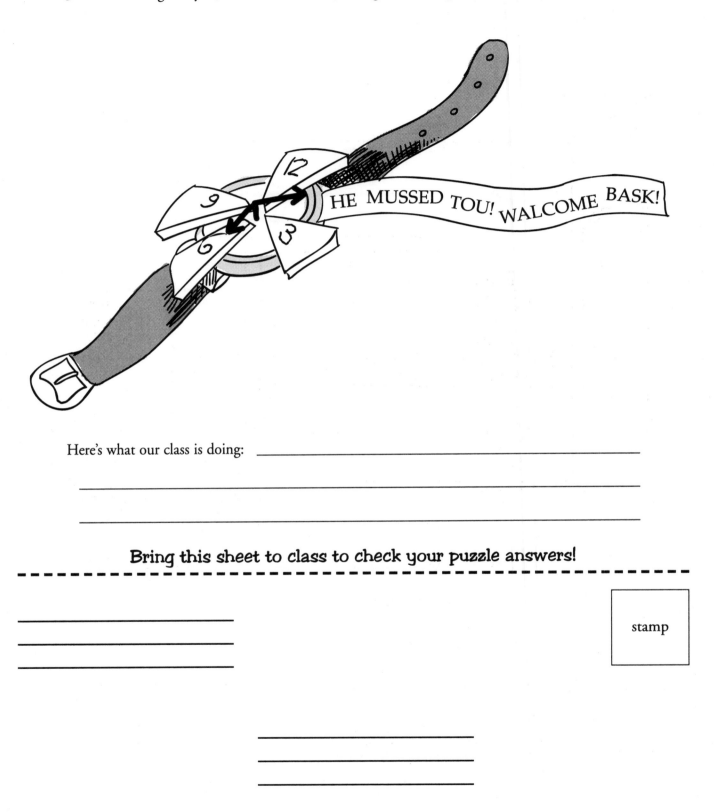

HE MUSSED TOU! WALCOME BASK!

Here's what our class is doing: _____

_____

_____

Bring this sheet to class to check your puzzle answers!

- -

_____

_____

_____

stamp

_____

_____

_____

What's Wrong with This Picture?

It's Sunday school time! But some things just don't look right, do they? Circle what is wrong.

Wrong or Right?

Use the Scripture in parentheses to answer the questions.

What do we call the wrong things that we do? (Romans 3:23; 6:23) _____

_____

How do we make things right with God? (1 John 1:9; John 3:16) _____

_____

*The thief comes only to steal and kill and destroy; I have come that they
may have life, and have it to the full.* John 10:10

What's wrong with our picture?

'Tis simple to say
We wish you were with us,
especially today!

Here's what our class is doing: _____

_____

_____

Bring this sheet to class to check your puzzle answers!

- -

_____

_____

_____

| | stamp |

_____

_____

_____

Animal Pairs

Do you know which animal is associated with each person? If you need help, look up the Bible verses in parentheses. Some people have an animal in common with someone else. See if you can find the pairs that go together.

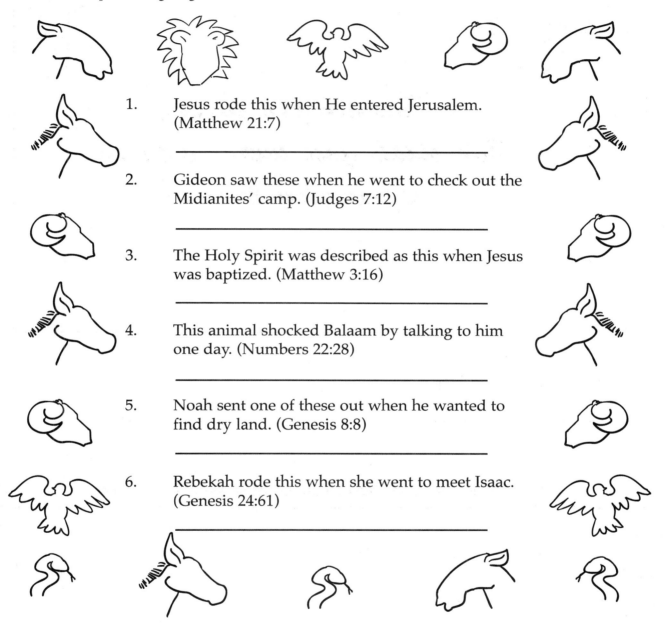

1. Jesus rode this when He entered Jerusalem. (Matthew 21:7)

   _____

2. Gideon saw these when he went to check out the Midianites' camp. (Judges 7:12)

   _____

3. The Holy Spirit was described as this when Jesus was baptized. (Matthew 3:16)

   _____

4. This animal shocked Balaam by talking to him one day. (Numbers 22:28)

   _____

5. Noah sent one of these out when he wanted to find dry land. (Genesis 8:8)

   _____

6. Rebekah rode this when she went to meet Isaac. (Genesis 24:61)

   _____

Which pairs go together?

Speaking of pairs, the old saying "two heads are better than one" fits today's Bible verse. Check it out!

Two are better than one, because they have a good return for their work: If one falls down, his friend can help him up. But pity the man who falls and has no one to help him up! Ecclesiastes 4:9-10

What's Missing?

Which letters are missing in the alphabet below? Finding the letters will tell you what's missing in our class.

A B C D E F G H I J K L

M N O P Q S T V W X Y Z

Here's what our class is doing: _____

_____

_____

Bring this sheet to class to check your puzzle answers!

- -

_____

_____

_____

stamp

_____

_____

_____

Congrats

A number of people are to be congratulated. But for what? See if you can sort out who receives which award. Draw a line from the award to the recipient.

Congratulations on your new baby!

Congratulations on your marriage

Congratulations on your new home

Congratulations on your new job

Elizabeth & Zechariah (Luke 1:57-66)

Abraham and Sarah (Genesis 21:1-6)

David (2 Samuel 5:4-5)

Gideon (Judges 6:12-16)

Esther (Esther 2:17-18)

Moses (Exodus 3:10)

Isaac & Rebekah (Genesis 24:67)

Joshua & Israelites (Joshua 11:23)

Rejoice with those who rejoice. Romans 12:15

Congratulations to you
for

_____

_____

_____

Good job!

Great!   **Excellent!**

Here's what our class is doing: _____

_____

_____

Bring this sheet to class to check your puzzle answers!

_____

_____

_____

stamp

_____

_____

_____

I...Forgot

Do you ever stick a note on your refrigerator to remember something important? Well, you're not the only one who has trouble remembering things. Some people in the Bible had the same problem. Think you know who they are and how they got in trouble? We'll see about that! Give yourself two points if you can remember what the person forgot. You get three points if you can remember the consequences of their actions. Write your answers next to each refrigerator magnet. Look up the Scripture if you need help.

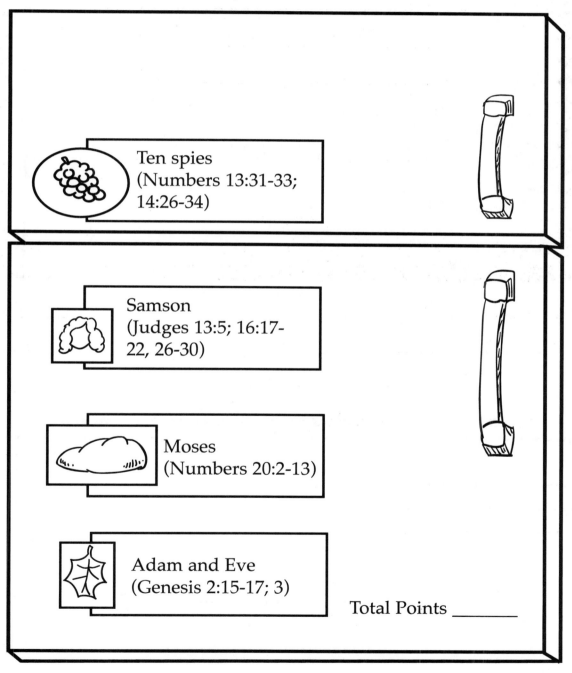

Ten spies
(Numbers 13:31-33; 14:26-34)

Samson
(Judges 13:5; 16:17-22, 26-30)

Moses
(Numbers 20:2-13)

Adam and Eve
(Genesis 2:15-17; 3)

Total Points _____

Do not forget my teaching, but keep my commands in your heart, for they will prolong your life many years and bring you prosperity. Proverbs 3:1-2

Don't Forget . . .

What _____

_____

When _____

_____

Where _____

Here's what our class is doing: _____

_____

_____

Bring this sheet to class to check your puzzle answers!

- -

_____

_____

_____

stamp

_____

_____

_____

"Times" to Remember

In order to do algebra, you've got to know multiplication. That's funny…in order to know the Bible verse, you need to know multiplication, too! For each letter of the alphabet, the product is given, just multiply to find out which letter is needed. Get it? Good! (Not every letter is shown. Of those shown, you may not use every letter.)

A	B	C	D	E	F	G	H	I	L	M
1x2	4x2	5x7	0x9	8x8	4x4	1x11	3x6	4x8	8x6	6x7

N	O	P	R	S	T	U	W	Y	Z
8x5	10x2	5x3	7x2	7x7	5x2	11 x4	5x5	3x3	9x9

0 20   40   20 10   16   20 14 11 64 10   10   20
__ __   __   __ __   __   __ __ __ __ __   __   __

0 20   11   20 20 0   2   40 0   10   20
__ __   __   __ __ __   __   __ __   __   __

49 18 2   14 64   25 32 10 18   20 10 18 64 14 49
__ __ __ __ __   __ __ __ __   __ __ __ __ __ __,

16   20 14   25   32 10 18   49   44   35   18
__   __ __   __   __ __ __   __   __   __   __

49   2   35   14 32 16 32 35 64 49   11   20 0
__   __ __   __ __ __ __ __ __ __   __   __ __

32 49   15   48 64   2   49 64 0
__ __   __   __ __   __   __ __ __   . Hebrews 13:16

Remember This

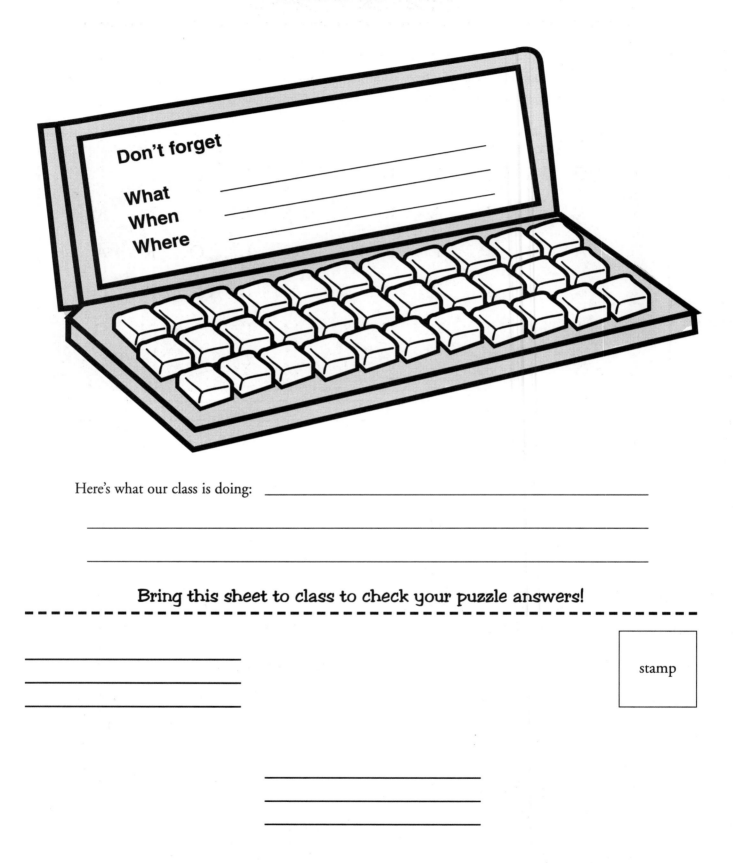

Don't forget

What _____

When _____

Where _____

Here's what our class is doing: _____

_____

_____

Bring this sheet to class to check your puzzle answers!

_____

_____

_____

stamp

_____

_____

_____

Friends of Jesus

There were many people who walked with Jesus. Some were disciples. Some later became disciples after He went back to heaven. Names can be found across, down, backward and diagonally. How many names can you find?

```
B  E  K  U  L  A  Z  A  R  U  S
C  A  T  M  U  N  H  O  J  I  T
S  N  R  A  R  E  T  E  P  Y  H
A  D  P  T  P  A  U  L  O  R  A
B  R  H  T  H  T  N  D  P  A  D
A  E  I  H  N  O  M  I  S  M  D
N  W  L  E  J  M  L  Y  D  I  A
R  B  I  W  S  A  M  O  H  T  E
A  C  P  A  H  T  R  A  M  W  U
B  K  J  S  E  M  A  J  R  E  S
L  E  A  N  A  H  T  A  N  K  W
```

Andrew	Lazarus	Mary	Philip
Barnabas	Luke	Matthew	Simon
Batholomew	Lydia	Nathanael	Thaddaeus
James	Mark	Paul	Thomas
John	Martha	Peter	

Read John 15:1-15. What does Jesus want His friends to do? _____

_____

Are you a friend of Jesus? How do you know? _____

_____

You are my friends if you do what I command. John 15:14

We want YOU

To: _____

Where: _____

When: _____

Time: _____

Here's what our class is doing: _____

_____

_____

Bring this sheet to class to check your puzzle answers!

_____
_____
_____

stamp

_____
_____
_____

Who Am I? Bible Hunt

Read the clues. How many do you need before you guess who the person is? If you can guess the person on the first clue, give yourself 10 points. Second clue — 5 points. Third clue — 1 point.

1.

Clue 1:   I went to Jesus for help when a member of my family was sick.
Clue 2:   I had to push through a large crowd to get to Him.
Clue 3:   Jesus healed my daughter in my own house!
          (Mark 5:22-24; 35-43)

2.

Clue 1:   When I was sick my sisters went to Jesus for help.
Clue 2:   I was dead; Jesus raised me to life.
Clue 3:   I had been in the grave for 4 days.
          (John 11)

3.

Clue 1:   I told Jesus that He was the Christ.
Clue 2:   When Jesus wanted to wash my feet, I said, "No way!"
Clue 3:   I denied Jesus three times.
          (Matthew 16:16; John 13:3-8; Matthew 26:33-34)

Do your best to present yourself to God as one approved, a workman who does not need to be ashamed and who correctly handles the word of truth. 2 Timothy 2:15

Books of the Bible Quiz

Some valuable books are missing from this collection. Do you know which ones are missing?

OLD TESTAMENT

Genesis

Leviticus

Numbers

Deuteronomy

Joshua

Judges

Ruth

2 Samuel

2 Kings

1 Chronicles

Ezra

Nehemiah

Esther

Job

Psalms

Ecclesiastes

Song of Solomon

Isaiah

Jeremiah

Lamentations

Ezekiel

Daniel

Joel

Amos

Jonah

Micah

Nahum

Habakkuk

Zephaniah

Haggai

Malachi

NEW TESTAMENT

Matthew

Luke

John

Romans

1 Corinthians

2 Corinthians

Galatians

Philippians

Colossians

2 Thessalonians

1 Timothy

2 Timothy

Titus

Hebrews

James

1 Peter

1 John

2 John

Jude

Revelation

Studying the Word of God is one way to become familiar with the books of the Bible.

Here's what our class is doing: _____

_____

_____

Bring this sheet to class to check your puzzle answers!

- -

_____

_____

_____

stamp

_____

_____

_____

That's What Friends Are For?

So you think you're a pretty good friend, huh? Take the following quiz and find out. Circle your answer.

1. A friend tells you to lie for him or her. You
A. Say, "Okay."
B. Say, "No way."
C. Say, "Someday, but not today."

2. A friend needs you to help him or her cheat on a test. You
A. Say, "Okay."
B. Say, "No way."
C. Say, "Someday, but not today."

3. A friend asks you to play a mean trick on another kid. You
A. Say, "Okay."
B. Say, "No way."
C. Say, "Someday, but not today."

Okay, those were easy. Let's see how you do on these:

4. A friend doesn't believe in Christ and thinks Christians are wimps. You've been trying to talk to her about Christ. You
A. Pretend you agree with her, so she won't get mad at you.
B. Tell her where you stand with Jesus.
C. Drop her as a friend immediately.

5. A friend lied to his parents and wants you to back him up on the lie. You
A. Tell your friend that you'll do it this time, but not next time.
B. Tell your friend that you refuse to lie for him.
C. Tell your friend he's stupid for lying.

6. A friend stole money from her brother and wants to borrow money from you to pay it back before her brother notices. You
A. Give her the money.
B. Give her the money, but only if she agrees to tell her brother what she did.
C. Refuse to help her at all.

If you answered:
    all A's — take a look at the Bible verse below and 1 Corinthians 13:4-7.
    all B's — you're a great friend, one who follows the Bible verse below.
    all C's — you need to remember that Jesus was a compassionate and wise friend. Take a look at the Bible verse below and 1 Corinthians 13:4-7.

A friend loves at all times. Proverbs 17:17

Isaiah 53

Want to know what a real friend does? Take a look at this passage from Isaiah (53:2-6). Jesus is the friend referred to in the passage. What is your response to what He did for you?

He grew up before him like a tender shoot, and like a root out of dry ground. He had no beauty or majesty to attract us to him, nothing in his appearance that we should desire him. He was despised and rejected by men, a man of sorrows, and familiar with suffering. Like one from whom men hide their faces he was despised, and we esteemed him not. Surely he took up our infirmities and carried our sorrows, yet we considered him stricken by God, smitten by him, and afflicted. But he was pierced for our transgressions, he was crushed for our iniquities; the punishment that brought us peace was upon him, and by his wounds we are healed. We all, like sheep, have gone astray, each of us has turned to his own way; and the Lord has laid on him the iniquity of us all.

Here's what our class is doing: _____

_____

_____

Bring this sheet to class to check your puzzle answers!

_____

_____

_____

stamp

_____

_____

_____

C Word Search

If you can "C" your way clear, you'll be able to find all of the words in the list in this puzzle.

```
                T   C   G
                O   H   O
                O   I   D
    B   O   B   C   R   E   A   T   I   O   N
    C   R   U   C   I   F   I   X   I   O   N
    O   O   S   A   H   P   A   I   A   C   Z
    N   C   T   S   I   R   H   C   A   I   N
                Y   I   C
                E   E   R
                S   S   U
                N   T   H
                A   R   C
                A   A   A
                N   S   L
                A   E   E
                C   A   B
                Q   C   N
```

Words:

Christ
Caesar
Caiaphas
Cain
Caleb
Canaan
chief priest
church
creation
crucifixion

Cast all your anxiety on him because he cares for you. 1 Peter 5:7

Words That Start with "C"

Creamed corn and crinkle-cut fries

Crispy cucumbers too

I like words that start with C.

How 'bout you?

Try to think of as many words that start with C as you can in 30 seconds. Ready? Go! Write them in the space below.

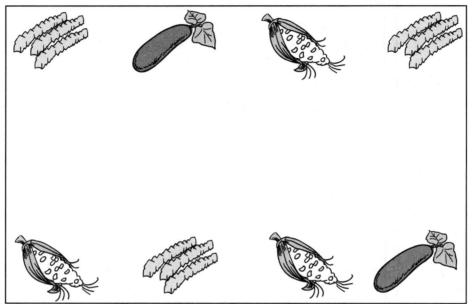

Here's what our class is doing: _____

_____

_____

Bring this sheet to class to check your puzzle answers!

_____

_____

_____

stamp

_____

_____

_____

86

A Monument to Missionaries

Many men and women faithfully carried the Gospel all over the world, as Jesus instructed. This was not an easy task. Many people were killed for the cause of Christ. There are no monuments dedicated to missionaries. But they are heroes of the faith all the same. Hidden in the word search below are the names of seventeen missionaries. How many can you find?

```
G E O R G E W H I T E F I E L D Q R N P
H L N B A R N E P O O L I S U B N A E R
A U T O X Q W I L L I A M C A R E Y T I
R T D S T X A Y Z Q H O T R P Q I S S S
R E Y S Y S E A S O N S N E E U M I N C
I J O Y O U G Y N A M A T Y E R A L A I
S D E R U N O N O T B E E W W T D N O L
O R D N D T A V I A R T I A A E R E O L
N A U D E O I N S V D A E R R R E R L A
A W Y W A L D E D L I L Y R E M H M B A
M L I W I L A L G M F L O I C A T E O N
A Y I V E V O D U R A Y D O H N A N B D
H A E S T B E N G O T R A I O Y F L J A
A S F R A I S I L A S D I Y V O P E I Q
R Y L I G O B E F O M R E A O A R A M U
G D W I G H T M O O D Y L W T U D V E I
Y A Y L W E R D Z O O M R R L A K E L L
L L M A D E M O O R E S I A A Y Y S L A
L G S C O M E F O L L C O W M M E L I H
I E A J O H N M A R K N D I W I A O O Y
B L L G I V A S E R E T R E H T O M T R
```

Gladys Aylward
Barnabas
William Carey
Jim Elliot
Father Damien
Billy Graham

John Mark
David Livingstone
Mary Magdalene
Mother Teresa
Patrick (Saint)
Paul

Peter
Priscilla and Aquila
Silas
Hudson and Maria Taylor
George Whitefield

Go into all the world and preach the good news to all creation. Mark 16:15

Modern Missionaries

Missionaries are still spreading the Gospel. What do you know about the missionaries your church supports? Check out the info below. You can support them by praying for them.

_____

_____

_____

_____

_____

On the lines below, write something you would like to tell a kid whose parents are serving as missionaries in another country. Consider getting the address of a missionary family and sending a letter.

_____

_____

_____

_____

_____

Here's what our class is doing: _____

_____

_____

Bring this sheet to class to check your puzzle answers!

- -

_____

_____

_____

| stamp |

_____

_____

_____

Calling Dr. God

Many people went to God when they had problems. Can you match the person with the problem? Draw a line from the person to the problem he or she had.

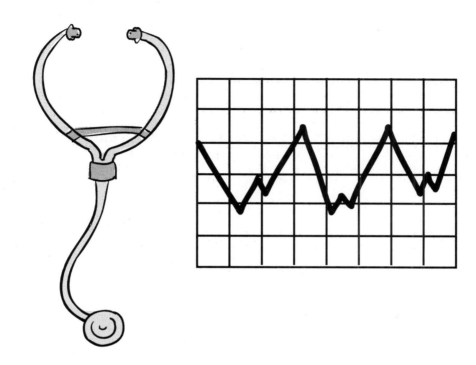

Person	**Problem**
Simon Peter's mother-in-law	almost died; prayed to live (2 Kings 20:1-11)
Hezekiah	had a fever (Mark 1:30-31)
Paul	couldn't see (Mark 8:22-26)
Elijah	was sick; died (Mark 5:21-24; 35-43)
Ten men	cured of illness (Luke 7:1-10)
Man lowered through roof	thorn in the flesh (2 Cor. 12:7-9)
Man at Bethsaida	was sad; God helped him (1 Kings 19:1-18)
Jairus's daughter	couldn't walk (Mark 2:1-12)
Man at Pool of Bethesda	went to Jesus with leprosy (Luke 17:11-19)
Centurion's servant	sick for 38 years (John 5:1-9)

I lift up my eyes to the hills — where does my help come from?
My help comes from the Lord, the Maker of heaven and earth. Psalm 121:1-2

Reaching for Recovery

Everyone you just read about had to reach out to God for help. Prayer is a way to reach out to God. Use the prayer starter below to lift your requests to Him.

God:

I need Your help with

_____

_____

I'm counting on You to

_____

_____

In Jesus' name. Amen.

Here's what our class is doing: _____

_____

_____

Bring this sheet to class to check your puzzle answers!

_____
_____
_____

stamp

_____
_____
_____

Sunday School Picnic

Circle all the things in the picture that begin with the letter P.

Speaking of the letter P, can you think of all the books of the Bible that begin with the letter P? (No peeking at your Bible, unless you're really stumped!)

_____

_____

_____

In the beginning God created the heavens and the earth. Genesis 1:1

Promises, Promises

The Bible has a lot of promises that contain words that begin with the letter P. God promises peace, His power, His protection, and He promises to provide for His people. Here are just a few of His promises.

Peace I leave with you; my peace I give you. I do not give to you as the world gives. Do not let your hearts be troubled and do not be afraid. (John 14:27)

You will keep in perfect peace him whose mind is steadfast, because he trusts in you. (Isaiah 26:3)

Now I know that the Lord saves his anointed; he answers him from his holy heaven with the saving power of his right hand. (Psalm 20:6)

You are my hiding place; you will protect me from trouble and surround me with songs of deliverance. (Psalm 32:7)

When you are tempted, [God] will also provide a way out so that you can stand up under it. (1 Corinthians 10:13)

Here's what our class is doing: _____

_____

_____

Bring this sheet to class to check your puzzle answers!

- -

_____

_____

_____

stamp

_____

_____

_____

Answers

page 9

Day 1: day and night created

Day 2: sky created

Day 3: land, waters, plants and trees created

Day 4: sun, moon and stars created

Day 5: birds and fish created

Day 6: land animals and people created

page 11

clockwise from bottom left: hailstorm, plague on livestock, darkness, boils on people and animals, flies, gnats and locusts, death of the firstborn, river to blood, frogs

page 12

40 days, 40 years, 300, 6 days

page 13

Across

1. Moses   4. Abraham   5. Jonah   6. David

8. Barak

Down

2. Sarah   3. Saul   4. Aaron   5. Jonathan

7. Miriam

page 14

The twelve disciples: Simon Peter, Andrew, James, John, Philip, Bartholomew, Thomas, Matthew, James son of Alphaeus, Thaddaeus, Simon the Zealot and Judas Iscariot.

The ten plagues: river to blood; frogs; gnats; flies; plague on livestock; boils on men and animals; hailstorm; locusts; –darkness; and death of the firstborn.

The twelve tribes of Israel: Reuben, Simeon, Judah, Issachar, Zebulun, Ephraim (1/2 tribe), Manasseh (1/2 tribe), Benjamin, Dan, Asher, Gad and Naphtali.

Consult Bible for list of Old and New Testament books.

Some of Jesus' miracles: healed a man with leprosy (Mark 1:40-42); healed a man at the pool of Bethesda (John 5:1-9); calmed a storm (Matthew 8:23-27); turned water into wine (John 2:1-11); raised Lazarus from the dead (John 11); raised Jairus's daughter from the dead (Mark 5:22-24; 38-42); fed 5,000 people (John 6:5-13); healed ten men of leprosy (Luke 17:11-19); healed a paralyzed man (Mark 2:3-12); healed a man's withered hand (Matthew 12:10-13).

page 15

Spear: The picture showing Saul hurling a javelin represents one of the many times Saul tried to kill David, who often entertained Saul by playing his harp (1 Samuel 19:9-10).

My best friend and me: The picture of David's best friend shows his friendship with Jonathan, Saul's son (1 Samuel 20).

Saul's robe: The cut robe represents how David spared Saul's life, even though Saul wanted to kill David (1 Samuel 24:3-4).

My slingshot: The sling with 5 rocks represents David's battle with Goliath (1 Samuel 17).

Oil: Samuel pouring oil on David's head represents David's anointing as Israel's future king (1 Samuel 16).

Crown: The crown represents David's finally becoming king of Israel (2 Samuel 5:4).

page 16

shepherd — Psalm 23:1; John 10:11

bread — Exodus 16:4; John 6:35; 2 Corinthians 11:23-24

light — Exodus 13:21; John 8:12

water — Exodus 17:6; John 4:14

page 17

A bush was on fire, not a lake.

Moses' staff turned into a snake, not his cloak.

page 18

Words unscrambled are: Rephidim, Manna, Jethro, Sinai and Tabernacle.

page 19

Trust in the Lord with all your heart. Proverbs 3:5

page 20

Wish U Were Here

page 21

A hand suddenly appeared and wrote on the wall.

Possible answers: amp; are; arm; came; camp; can; car; care; carp; era; man; many; mar; name; nay; per; perm; pray; ram; ramp; ran; ray; rep; yam; yarn.

page 23

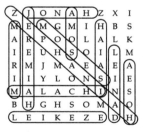

page 24

partial list of possible answers: air, ant, arch, chain, chair, chant, chastity, chat, chin, hair, hay, hint, his, icy, inch, itch, rain, ran, ranch, rant, saint, sanity, shanty, stain, stair, star, starch, tan, tin, tiny, titan, train, trinity, tryst, sit, sat

page 27

1. water; 2. heal his servant; 3. because it was the Sabbath; 4. heal her daughter; 5. He was blind; 6. He fed 5,000 people; 7. through the roof; 8. brought her son back to life (Luke 7:11-15); 9. He walked on water; 10. He calmed a storm; 11. one; 12. at the Pool of Bethesda

page 28
Jesus Christ is the same yesterday and today and forever. Hebrews 13:8

page 29
Do
store up treasure in heaven, seek first God's kingdom
Don't
store up treasure on earth, serve two masters, worry

page 30
1. a Bible and a shirt   2. train track
3. diamond   4. The skates were next to the bed.

page 31
1. Macedonia
2. strengthen you, Iconium, Lystra, Lystra, Antioch, Iconium, Philippi, girl, Thessalonica

page 32
Adam and Eve; Isaac and Rebekah; Cain killed Abel; Abraham and Sarah; Joseph and Benjamin; Joshua and Caleb; Moses and Aaron; Mary and Martha; Saul and David

page 35
1. EARTHQUAKE
2. MARY
3. PETER
4. JOHN
5. BURIAL CLOTH
6. THOMAS
7. ANGEL
8. STONE
9. GUARDS
10. EMMAUS

```
T O G O D (P E T E R) W
(H T O L C L A I R U B
 O H O L Y M R A J A M
 G O D Z M S T O N E K
 T M G A S M H O L Y N
 M A U N U N Q N Y V X
 B S A W A E U R Z O O
 J A R R M W A N G E L
 L A D E M M K N O W S
 I S S U E D E F O R E
```

page 36
DEATH, HEATH, HEAT, HEAR, DEAR, BEAR, BEAT, BENT, DENT, LENT, LINT, LIFT, LIFE
SOUR, SOUL, SOUP, SOAP, SOAR, SEAR, WEAR, SWEAR, SWEAT, SWEET
EARLY, EARL, EARN, LEARN, LEAN, MEAN, MANE, MATE, LATE

page 37
Across
1. Peter   2. Barabbas   5. Judas
Down
1. Pilate   3. Mary   4. Caiaphas

page 38
FOR YOU

page 41
hat on snowman, scarf on girl by snowman, pants on skating girl, hat on skating boy, skirt on skating girl, missing sack on bench, colored headband on skating girl.

page 43
I have loved you with an everlasting love; I have drawn you with loving-kindness. Jeremiah 31:3

page 45
Answer: "If you knew who asks you for a drink, you'd ask me for living water."
Question/Comment: "How can you ask me for a drink?"

Answer: "The water I will give will become a spring of water."
Question/Comment: "Are you greater than our father Jacob, who gave us this well?"

Answer: "I have no husband."
Question/Comment: "Go call your husband."

Answer: "I who speak to you am he."
Question/Comment: "I know the Messiah is coming."

The woman told everyone to come and see Jesus, the Messiah.

Bonus Round: How can a person become new? Or: What happens when a person follows Christ.

page 46
WINTER, WINNER, SINNER, SPINNER, SPLINTER, SPLINT, SPRINT, SPRING
SEED, REED, READ, LEAD, PLEAD, PLAID, PLAIN, PLANT

page 47
"Our cameras show the statue the king built. It's 85 feet tall." should be edited to "Our cameras show the statue the king built. It's 90 feet tall."
"When musical instruments are played, everyone is to bow down and worship the statue of King Nebuchadnezzar" is correct.
"The king's wise men reported that Shadrach, Meshach and Abednego refused to worship the statue" is correct.
"The king told Shadrach, Meshach, and Abednego that they'd be thrown into the lions' den if they didn't bow down to the statue." should be edited to "The king told Shadrach, Meshach and Abednego that they'd be thrown into the fiery furnace if they didn't bow down to the statue."
"The king gave them one more chance to bow down. They told him they would bow down." should be edited to "The king gave them one more chance to bow down. They told him they would not bow down."
How the story ended: Shadrach, Meshach and Abednego were

thrown into the fiery furnace. The king saw four men instead of the three that he had thrown in. Shadrach, Meshach and Abednego were taken out of the furnace. They king saw that they weren't harmed.

page 49
Across
1. Nehemiah; 6. clear; 7. priest; 9. law; 10. book
Down
2. Ezra; 3. Israel; 4. watergate; 5. scribe; 8. stood; 11. noon

Page 50
1. head in the clouds; 2. head over heels in love; 3. a good head on your shoulders; 4. keep your head above water; 5. in over your head; 6. head for the hills; 7. it's all in your head; 8. at the head of the class

page 51
1-D (Eutychus fell out of a window); 2-E (Jonah was thrown into the sea); 3-A (Jeremiah was thrown into a well); 4-B (Daniel was thrown into the lions' den); 5-F (Paul was shipwrecked).

page 52
The word FALL appears 21 times.

page 53
one leper: HEALING; Solomon: TEMPLE; Jacob: GOD'S PRESENCE; Anna & Simeon: MESSIAH; David: RETURN OF THE ARK

page 55
Today in the town of David a Savior has been born to you; he is Christ the Lord. Luke 2:11

page 56
wreath/girl with obvious teeth, books/girl with hooks on her shirt, socks/boy with clocks, bears/boy with chairs

page 57

page 61
Hospitable: Rahab, Abraham/Sarah, David, Abigail, Jonathan, Solomon, Boaz.
Not hospitable: Saul, Nabal, Pharaoh.
page 63
A. 5; B. 2, 3; C. 4; D. 1

page 65
Nobody cares about me. (I will never leave you nor forsake you. Joshua 1:5)
Why are you always using my stuff? Get out! (A gentle answer turns away wrath, but a harsh word stirs up anger. Proverbs 15:1)
I have the best grade in the whole class. (Let him who boasts boast in the Lord. 1 Corinthians 1:31)

page 66
Easy - Judas (John 18:2); Adam and Eve (Genesis 2:20, 3:20); tree of the knowledge of good and evil (Genesis 2:16-17)
Medium Hard - Simon Peter (John 18:10); farmer (Genesis 4:2); The Midianites (Judges 6:11-14)
Super Hard - Malchus (John 18:10); trumpets and empty jars with torches inside (Judges 7:15-16)
Impossible - Enoch and Elijah (Genesis 5:24; 2 Kings 2:11)

page 67
Answers will vary. Some suggested answers:
Simon: between cold and warmer; "Sinful" woman: warm; Zacchaeus: warm; Martha: warm; Lydia: warm; Cornelius: warm; Barnabas: warm; Disciples: cold.

page 68
WE MISSED YOU! WELCOME BACK!

page 69
What's wrong: teacher has on two different shoes; upside-down writing on the chalkboard; one kid has a tennis racquet; clock with backward numbers; one kid has on skates instead of shoes; raccoon is sitting in a chair; one kid is asleep; one kid is wearing a coat; one kid is missing paper while the other kids have paper.
What do we call the wrong things that we do? Sin.
How do we make things right with God? Admit we have sin and accept Jesus' death on the cross as payment for our sin.

page 71
Pairs that match: 1 and 4 (donkey); 2 and 6 (camel); 3 and 5 (dove)

page 72
"What's Missing?" — UR (You are!)

page 73
New baby: Elizabeth & Zechariah; Abraham and Sarah
New job: David (king); Gideon (judge of the Israelites); Moses (as leader of the Israelites)
Marriage: Esther; Isaac & Rebekah
New home: Joshua & Israelites (the promised land)

page 75

Person	What He/She Forgot	Consequences
Ten spies	God said he'd give them land	Couldn't enter promised land; wandered 40 years
Samson	To avoid having hair cut	Captured; lost sight; lost life eventually
Moses	To speak to rock	Couldn't enter promised land
Adam & Eve	God said don't eat from the Tree of the Knowledge of Good and Evil	Thrown out of the garden; sin came into the world

page 77

Do not forget to do good and to share with others, for with such sacrifices God is pleased. Hebrews 13:16

page 79

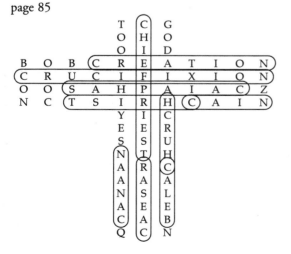

LOVE EACH OTHER

page 81

1. Jairus   2. Lazarus   3. Peter

page 82

Old Testament: Exodus, 1 Samuel, 1 Kings, 2 Chronicles, Proverbs, Hosea, Obadiah, Zechariah
New Testament: Mark, Acts, Ephesians, 1 Thessalonians, Philemon, 2 Peter, 3 John

page 85

page 86

Answers could include: cab, cob, column, cute, club, cool, Christmas, cap, candy, cane, etc.

page 87

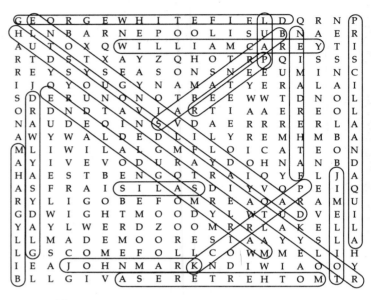

page 89

Simon Peter's mother-in-law	had a fever
Hezekiah	almost died
Paul	thorn in the flesh
Elijah	was sad
ten men	went to Jesus with leprosy
Man lowered through roof	couldn't walk
Man at Bethsaida	couldn't see
Jairus's daughter	was sick; died
Man at pool of Bethesda	sick for 38 years
centurion's servant	cured of illness

page 91

people; picnic table; picnic table benches; pizza; punch; punch bowl; pastor; purse; picnic basket
Books of the Bible that begin with P: Psalms, Proverbs, Philippians, Philemon, 1 & 2 Peter